BEETHOVEN

MW01132273

15 VARIATIONS AND A FUGUE IN E-FLAT MAJOR
("Eroica Variations") OPUS 35
FOR THE PIANO

EDITED BY CHARLES TIMBRELL

AN ALFRED MASTERWORK EDITION

Copyright © 2014 by Alfred Music
All rights reserved.   Printed in USA.
ISBN-10: 1-4706-1984-9
ISBN-13: 978-1-4706-1984-8

To Stewart Gordon, admired teacher,
pianist, author, and editor

Cover art: Heiligenstadt (*19th century*) *Anonymous*

LUDWIG VAN BEETHOVEN

Contents

Foreword

ABOUT THIS EDITION

This edition is based on the autograph, which was completed October 1802, and is located at the Beethoven-Archiv in Bonn, Germany. The autograph served as the source-score for the first edition, which was published by Breitkopf & Härtel in August 1803 in Leipzig, Germany (plate number 167). Both sources have been compared with the first complete Beethoven edition (*Gesamtausgabe*, 1862–65) and later editions by Hans von Bülow, Adam Carse, Peter Hauschild, Sigmund Lebert, Erwin Ratz, Adolf Ruthardt, and Joseph Schmidt-Görg.

In this edition, all parenthetical material is editorial.

Regarding articulations, Beethoven's distinctions between dots and wedges are often inconsistent and ambiguous. This edition follows the prevalent modern tradition of using dots only.

Beethoven's rare pedal indications are the only ones given, and performers should base their pedaling on their own stylistic awareness, the sonority of the piano, and the acoustics of the performance venue. A few comments regarding pedaling are found in the "Performance Suggestions" section that follows.

Portrait of Ludwig van Beethoven (1803),
Christian Horneman (1765–1844), Danish

15 Variations and a Fugue in E-flat Major, Op. 35
Edited by Charles Timbrell

HISTORICAL BACKGROUND

Ludwig van Beethoven (1770–1827) composed the *15 Variations and a Fugue in E-flat Major*, Op. 35, in the summer and fall of 1802. The work occupies a prominent place in the piano literature due to its structural grandeur and the originality and beauty of its piano writing. Chronologically, it holds a central position in the composer's variation writing, coming after numerous earlier sets (composed before 1800) and before his monumental late masterpiece, the *33 Variations on a Waltz by Diabelli*, Op. 120 (composed in 1823).[1]

Preliminary sketches for Op. 35 appear in the Kessler sketchbook, which Beethoven maintained throughout the year 1802. In a pioneering study of this notebook, noted Beethoven scholar Gustav Nottebohm (1817–1882) concluded that Beethoven first intended to compose a conventional set of variations, only realizing while working out the material that he should write something more serious and substantial.[2] Later and more extensive sketches for Op. 35 are found in the Wielhorsky sketchbook, alongside those for the "Eroica" Symphony.[3]

The "Eroica Variations"—so-called because they were later re-worked for the finale of his Third ("Eroica") Symphony, Op. 55—were written while Beethoven was staying in the quiet Vienna suburb of Heiligenstadt, where his doctor suggested he might get relief from his hearing problems. The bold, cheerful, and often humorous variations contain little hint of the personal torment that Beethoven felt at the time, which he expressed in a celebrated letter to his brothers, dated October 6, 1802. Known as the *Heiligenstadt Testament*, the letter dwells on the terrible knowledge Beethoven had been keeping to himself for some time—that he was becoming deaf:

How could I possibly refer to the impairing *of a sense* which in me should be more perfectly developed than in other people, a sense which at one time I possessed in the greatest perfection.…My misfortune pains me doubly, inasmuch as it leads to my being misjudged. For me there can be no relaxation in human society, no refined conversations, no mutual confidences. I must live like an outcast.… [During the last six months] I was on the point of putting an end to my life. The only thing that held me back was my art. For indeed it seemed to me impossible to leave this world before I had produced all the works that I felt the urge to compose.[4]

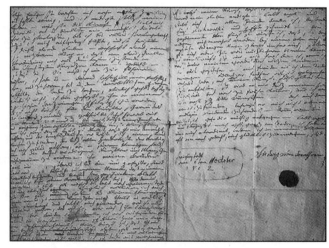

A facsimile of the Heiligenstadt Testament

Two weeks later, in a better frame of mind, Beethoven wrote the publishers Breitkopf & Härtel in Leipzig:

I have composed two sets of Variations [Opp. 34 and 35] that are worked out in quite a *new manner*, and each in a *separate and different* way. I would infinitely prefer to have them engraved by you.… Usually I have to wait for other people to tell me when I have new ideas, because I never know this myself. But this time I myself can assure you that in both these works *the method is quite new*.[5]

---

1 Beethoven's early sets of variations are numbered WoO 64–77. WoO is an abbreviation for *Werke ohne Opuszahl* (works without opus number) in the catalogue of Beethoven's complete works: Georg Kinsky, *Das Werk Beethovens: thematisch-bibliographisches Verzeichnis seiner sämtlichen vollendeten Kompositionen*, completed and ed. Hans Halm (Munich: G. Henle, 1955).

2 Gustav Nottebohm, *Ein Skizzenbuch von Beethoven* (Leipzig: Breitkopf & Härtel, 1865), 32.

3 Christopher Reynolds, "Beethoven's Sketches for the Variations in E-flat, Op. 35," *Beethoven Studies 3* (New York: Cambridge University Press, 1982), 47–84.

4 *The Letters of Beethoven*, Vol. 3, ed. and trans. Emily Anderson (London: St. Martin's Press, 1961), 1351–52.

5 *The Letters of Beethoven*, Vol. 1, 76–77.

It is possible that in the short time between these two documents, Beethoven had weathered his personal crisis and that composition of the Variations Opp. 34 and 35 relieved his anguished mood and helped him regain artistic resolve. In any case, the new style that he refers to, which has often been called his "heroic style" or "middle-period style," had indeed been developing at this time and would culminate in the following year with his imposing "Eroica" Symphony.

Breitkopf accepted both sets of variations in early November, but disagreement over the rights to publish another work, the String Quintet, Op. 29, caused Beethoven to delay sending the autographs until December. In June 1803, he reminded Breitkopf to include on the title page of Op. 35 the fact that the theme was from his ballet *The Creatures of Prometheus* (*Die Geschöpfe des Prometheus*, Op. 43)—a wish that was not granted; nor was his wish to receive proof copies. Opus 35 was finally published in August, with a dedication to Count Moritz Lichnowsky (1771–1837). According to Beethoven's stipulations, Opp. 34 and 35 became his first variations to be published with opus numbers.

In December 1803, Beethoven's student Ferdinand Ries (1784–1838) sent the publisher Nikolaus Simrock a list of nine errors in Breitkopf & Härtel's edition of Op. 35. If there was a hope that Simrock would publish his own edition, it was never achieved. Most of the errors cited by Ries are obvious ones that were corrected in various later publications.[6]

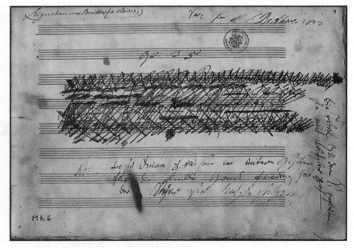

First page of the Eroica Variations

A lengthy and complimentary review of Op. 35 appeared in the Leipzig *Allgemeine musikalische Zeitung* on February 22, 1804. The critic wrote:

> Inexhaustible imagination, original humor, and deep, intimate, even passionate feeling are the particular features, as it were, from which arises the ingenious physiognomy that distinguishes nearly all of Herr van Beethoven's works. This earns him one of the highest places among instrumental composers of first rank, since particularly his latest works show unmistakably the care that he takes to maintain a chosen character and to combine the greatest freedom with purity of phrasing and, I would like to say, with contrapuntal elegance. All of the peculiarities of this composer just cited can be found to a very distinct degree in the work named above. Even the form of the whole, which deviates so far from what is customary, bears witness to unmistakable genius.[7]

The writer went on to praise various individual variations and to make some practical suggestions regarding hand positions, fingering, and voicing.

Many noted pianists during the 19th century performed the "Eroica Variations," including Johannes Brahms (1833–1897), Clara Schumann (1819–1896), Hans von Bülow (1830–1894), Franz Rummel (1853–1901), Conrad Ansorge (1862–1930), Ferruccio Busoni (1866–1924), and Artur Schnabel (1882–1951). Franz Liszt (1811–1886) taught it to Ansorge in a master class in 1886, and a number of Liszt's former students performed it in the early 20th century, including Eugen d'Albert (1864–1932), Berthe Marx-Goldschmidt (1859–1925), Karl Klindworth (1830–1916), Frederic Lamond (1868–1948), and Alfred Reisenauer (1863–1907).

---

6 Nikolaus Simrock, *Simrock-Jahrbuch*, Vol. 2 (Berlin: Simrock, 1929), 28–29.

7 *The Critical Reception of Beethoven's Compositions by His German Contemporaries*, Wayne M. Senner, ed. and trans., Robin Wallace and William Meredith, eds. (Lincoln: University of Nebraska, 1999), 190–95.

ABOUT THE MUSIC

The form of the "Eroica Variations" is unique in the history of variations. The work begins, not with the theme, but with a 64-measure introduction consisting of a 16-measure statement of the bass line of the theme (marked *Introduzione col basso del tema*) and three 16-measure variations of it (labeled *a due*, *a tre*, and *a quattro*, to indicate two, three, and four voices). Only then does the theme (*tema*) appear, also 16 measures long. Fifteen numbered variations follow, leading to the *Finale alla fuga*.

In the opening measures, the bass line begins pianissimo in half notes doubled at the octave and reaches an implied (unharmonized) half-cadence in measure 8. The second half starts with a measure of rest followed by three abrupt fortissimo eighth-note octaves, then a measure of rest, a fermata on the dominant, and a four-measure *codetta*. Each phrase is nicely characterized: the first by intervallic leaps that draw our attention; the second by half-steps that suggest playfulness; the third by the comically loud and abrupt octaves that are preceded and followed by questioning rests; and the fourth providing a reassuring answer.

The 15 variations that lie at the heart of the work are mostly "constant-harmony variations," in which the harmonic structure is fixed.[8] But the *tema* is also varied, and sometimes the bass and the *tema* are so melded that it is often difficult to say which is the "real theme."[9] The binary form of the bass line is adhered to throughout the variations, with Variations I–XIII using repeat signs and XIV and XV being through-composed, the latter with an eight-measure coda in which the *tema* is rhythmically varied in C minor (the relative minor) and ends on a quiet G major chord. The concluding three-voice fugue in the tonic E-flat (*Finale alla fugue*) foreshadows important formal features in the finale of the "Eroica" Symphony, where some of the contrapuntal writing is retained as well as such details as the staggered juxtaposition of the bass line and the *tema* from measures 62ff. This finale begins with a three-voice fugue built on the first four notes of the bass line (including, in measures 90ff., its inversion). The texture then becomes increasingly homophonic until the momentum is arrested by long, loud chords (measures 129–131). A short scale leads to a quiet re-statement of the *tema (Andante con moto)* followed by two unnumbered variations of it. The work closes strongly, with broken chords in the left hand and diminutions of a fragment of the theme in the right hand.

Beethoven used the *tema* in two previous compositions, both from 1801: the finale of his ballet *The Creatures of Prometheus* (*Die Geschöpfe des Prometheus*, Op. 43); and the seventh of his *12 Contredances for Orchestra* (*Zwölf Contretänze für Orchester*, WoO 14).

PERFORMANCE SUGGESTIONS

The technical demands of the "Eroica Variations" are considerable, on a par with many other works from Beethoven's middle period, including the Sonatas Opp. 31, 53, and 57. A brilliant finger technique is called for, and often the demands for speed and volume coincide. The ability to project the character of each variation is important, as is the overall pacing of the work. Some variations might be connected (Variations I–III, V and VI, and XI and XII) while others should be preceded by a short pause because of the change of mood or dynamics (Variations IV, VIII, X, XI, and XIV). Restrained expression is essential in Variations VIII, XIV, and XV, and a full appreciation of counterpoint is needed not only for the fugue but also for the canonical writing in Variation VII and the interplay of hands in Variation X.

The following performance suggestions may prove helpful:

Introduction, Theme, Vars. I–III (*Allegretto vivace*): This editor favors connecting the half notes in the Introduction and in all recurrences later in the work. However, since Beethoven never indicated the desired touch, it is possible to lightly detach these notes. Hans von Bülow suggests detachment in his edition,[10] and this advice is also given by Liszt[11] and Heinrich Schenker.[12]

---

8 Elaine Sisman, "Variation," *The New Harvard Dictionary of Music*, ed. Don Randel (Cambridge, MA: Harvard University Press, 1986), 903.

9 An interesting discussion of the origin of the *tema* is found in Elwood Derr, "Beethoven's Long-Term Memory of C.P.E. Bach's Rondo in E-flat, W. 61/1 (1787), Manifest in the Variations in E-flat for Piano, Opus 35 (1802)," *The Musical Quarterly* 70/1 (Winter 1984), 45–76.

10 *Beethoven. Variations for the Piano, Book I*, ed. Hans von Bülow and Sigmund Lebert (New York: G. Schirmer, 1898), 13.

11 *The Piano Master Classes of Franz Liszt: Diary Notes of August Göllerich*, ed. Richard Louis Zimdars (Bloomington: Indiana University Press, 1996), 135.

12 Nicholas Marston, "Notes to an Heroic Analysis: A Translation of Schenker's Unpublished Study of Beethoven's Piano Variations, Op. 35," *Nineteenth-Century Piano Music*, ed. David Witten (New York: Garland Publishing, 1997), 25.

Von Bülow also inserts a comma (like a breath mark in vocal music) after the fermata in measure 13 and at similar places throughout the work. This seems valid because of Beethoven's slurring of the following notes here and at equivalent later points.

Var. I: Legato and lyrical, with very little pedal. Here, and in the subsequent variations, slightly stress the bass line. The *sf* markings are within the context of *p*.

Var. II: The character is exuberant, with the notes well articulated and the pedaling shallow and precise.

Var. III: Be aware of the three registers at play within the *f* dynamic.

Var. IV: Play the left hand expressively but without rubato, with the right-hand chords soft and unaccented.

Var. V: Mozartean elegance is needed here, with the texture kept thin and the tempo steady. Use pedal in the second half, changing on each *sf*.

Var. VI: The difficult left-hand part must be very light and quiet, with the una corda pedal. The sound should be a bit veiled and mysterious, with minimal sustaining pedal. Release the una corda pedal in the last measure.

Var. VII: Play with a very precise touch in both hands, close to the keys, with a steady tempo and strong accents on each *sf*.

Var. VIII: The melody in the upper voice should sing *p* above the *pp* accompaniment, with dynamic nuances but without strong rubato. Try to control the balances without using the una corda pedal. Liszt told his student Conrad Ansorge that the tempo should be "not slow."[13]

Var. IX: The difficulties arise from the rapid changes of hand position, the constant staccatos, and the need to bring out the melody formed by the grace notes in the left hand. Practice the right hand in various rhythms and with the notes grouped according to the changes in hand position.

Var. X: Very playful and delicate, except for the brief *ff*.

Var. XI: The first half is a return to the Mozartean style of Var. V, but the last four measures are abrupt, with the grace notes coming before the beat.

Var. XII: The dynamic contrasts are between *p* and *f*, with *ff* only at the end. Use short thrusts of the hand, played close to the keys.

Var. XIII: The boisterous humor of this difficult variation might be enhanced by playing the grace notes together with the note that follows. By *sempre forte*, Beethoven indicates that the chords should be as loud as the notes that fall on the downbeats. Fast, rhythmic practice of the changes of hand position will be helpful for gaining accuracy (and these can be practiced *p*, to avoid strain).

Var. XIV: *Legatissimo* and *cantabile* throughout, with a warm and well-projected tone, without the una corda pedal. Let the final chord diminish completely, add a slight comma before the *Adagio*, and make a smooth elision into Var. XV.

Var. XV (*Largo*): This musically challenging variation should sound free throughout, almost as if it were improvised, with "breathing" space between phrases and with unexaggerated dynamics. The *p* in measures 4, 10, 12, 24, and 32 should be sudden. Crescendo is implied near the end of measures 8, 10, and 13. Use flutter pedal in measures 38–40. The fermata at the end should allow the sound to die away considerably before beginning the finale.

Finale alla Fuga (*Allegro con brio*): Make a short break after the last chord of Var. XV and begin the fugue simply and rather quietly. Clear voicing, rhythmic precision, and structural awareness are required throughout. In the long *ff* buildup on the dominant (mm. 111–131), vary the sonority slightly to avoid a prolonged percussiveness. The fermatas in measures 129–131 should not be too long, and the arpeggio in measure 130 should be fast. Pedal frequently in measures 133–140 and use flutter pedaling in measures 141–148. The *p* in measures 152 and 160 should be sudden, preceded by a lift of the pedal. In measures 172–180, some pianists play four-note chords in the left hand, doubling the bass line with the thumb and thus making the theme especially clear. During the closing pages, keep the dynamics under control; measures 159–204 should not rise much above *f*. This editor plays measures 196–205 somewhat more broadly than the preceding measures.

---

13 *The Piano Master Classes of Franz Liszt: Diary Notes of August Göllerich*, 135.

SOURCES CONSULTED

Anderson, Emily, ed. and trans. *The Letters of Beethoven*. New York: St. Martin's Press, 1961.

Cockshoot, John V. *The Fugue in Beethoven's Piano Music*. London: Routledge & Kegan, 1959.

Cooper, Barry, ed. *The Beethoven Compendium*. London: Thames and Hudson, 1991.

Derr, Ellwood. "Beethoven's Long-Term Memory of C.P.E. Bach's Rondo in E-flat, W. 61/1 (1787), Manifest in the Variations in E-flat for Piano, Opus 35 (1802)." *The Musical Quarterly* 70/1 (Winter 1984): 45–76.

Forbes, Elliot, ed. *Thayer's Life of Beethoven*, rev. ed. Princeton, NJ: Princeton University Press, 1967.

Kinsky, Georg. *Das Werk Beethovens: thematisch-bibliographisches Verzeichnis seiner sämtlichen vollendeten Kompositionen*, completed and ed. Hans Halm. Munich: G. Henle, 1955.

Marston, Nicholas. "Notes to an Heroic Analysis: A Translation of Schenker's Unpublished Study of Beethoven's Piano Variations, Op. 35." *Nineteenth-Century Piano Music*, ed. David Witten. New York: Garland Publishing, 1997: 15–52.

Nottebohm, Gustav. *Ein Skizzenbuch von Beethoven*, Leipzig: Breitkopf & Härtel, 1865.

Reynolds, Christopher. "Beethoven's Sketches for the Variations in E-flat, Op. 35." *Beethoven Studies 3*. New York: Cambridge University Press, 1982: 47–84.

Senner, Wayne M., trans. and ed., Robin Wallace and William Meredith, eds. *The Critical Reception of Beethoven's Compositions by His German Contemporaries*. Lincoln: University of Nebraska Press, 1999.

Simrock, Nikolaus. *Simrock-Jahrbuch*, Vol. 2. Berlin: Simrock, 1929.

Sipe, Thomas. *Beethoven. Eroica Symphony*. New York: Cambridge University Press, 1998.

Sisman, Elaine. "Variation." *The New Harvard Dictionary of Music*, ed. Don Randel. Cambridge, M.A.: Harvard University Press, 1986: 903.

Solomon, Maynard. *Beethoven*. New York: Schirmer Books, 1977.

Tovey, Donald Francis. "Beethoven: Fifteen Variations and Fugue, Op. 35." *Essays in Musical Analysis*, Vol. 6. London: Oxford University Press, 1939.

Zimdars, Richard Louis, ed. *The Piano Master Classes of Franz Liszt: Diary Notes of August Göllerich*. Bloomington: Indiana University Press, 1996.

The following editions were also consulted:

Beethovens Werke: Kritische Gesamtausgabe, Vol. 17 of 25. Leipzig: Breitkopf & Härtel, 1862–65.

Bülow, Hans von and Sigmund Lebert, eds. *Beethoven: Variations for the Piano, Book I*. New York: G. Schirmer, 1898.

Carse, Adam, ed. *Beethoven: Variations for Piano, Book II*. London: Augener, n.d. (ca. 1924).

Hauschild, Peter, ed. *Beethoven: Variationen für Klavier, Band I*. Frankfurt: C. F. Peters, 1970.

Lebert, Sigmund, ed. *Beethoven: 15 Variationen mit Fuge für das Pianoforte, Op. 35*. Stuttgart: Cotta, 1891.

Ruthardt, Adolf, ed. *Beethoven: Variationen für Klavier, Band I*. Frankfurt: Peters, n.d. (ca. 1905).

Ratz, Erwin, ed. *Beethoven: Variationen für Klavier, Band I*. 2nd ed. Vienna: Wiener Urtext Edition, 1973.

Schmidt-Görg, Joseph, ed. *Beethoven: Variationen für Klavier, Band II*. Munich: Henle, 1961.

ACKNOWLEDGEMENTS

I wish to thank E. L. Lancaster and Carol Matz for their expert editorial advice, and William Kloss for his valued suggestions.

Dedicated to Count Moritz Lichnowsky

15 Variations and a Fugue in E-flat Major
("Eroica Variations")

Ludwig van Beethoven (1770–1827)
Op. 35

(a) The lowest key on Beethoven's piano was F, but it is musically justifiable to play E-flat octaves in both endings of the theme.

(b) There is no staccato in this measure in the autograph and the first edition.

(e) The downbeats in the left hand in measures 2 and 4 are quarter notes in the autograph.

Canone all' ottava (canon at the octave)

VAR. VII

VAR. VIII

(g) Beethoven's pedal markings (measures 9–18).

VAR. X

20

VAR. XI

VAR. XII

(h) The *sf* is probably an error in the autograph and first edition.

(i) Possible facilitation:

Similarly in measures 8–11.

22

23

(k) The trill should be unmeasured and not too fast, counting the eighth-note beats
and ending with the sixteenth notes metrically in place.

① The trills should be unmeasured and not too fast, counting the eighth-note beats and ending
with the sixteenth notes metrically in place.

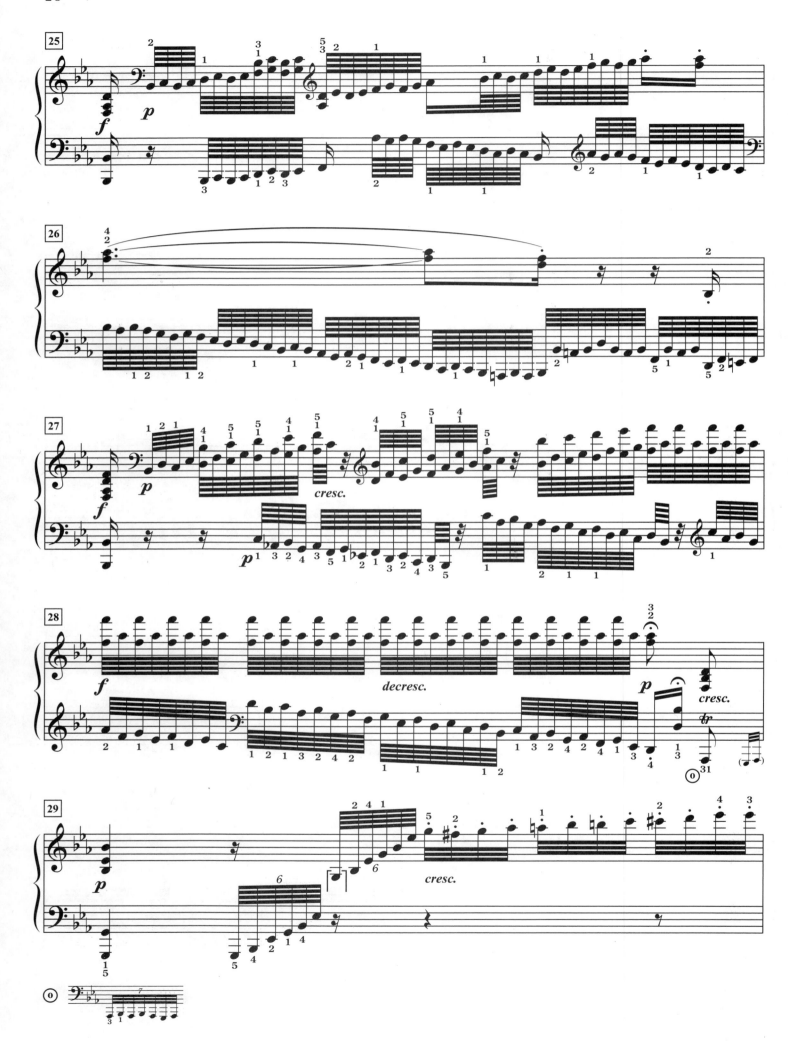

28

FINALE
Alla Fuga

(S) The natural sign on A is missing in the autograph and first edition.

(u)

(v)

(w)

(x) The arpeggio sign is continuous from bottom note to top in the autograph; in the first edition there are separate arpeggio signs for each hand.

(y) Beethoven's pedal markings.

(z) Left-hand chord as in the autograph; the first edition has C–E♭–F–A♭.

(aa) For measures 141–144, follow this pattern:

(bb) For measures 141–144, follow this pattern:

(cc) For measures 145–148 follow this pattern:

(dd) The lower fingering will help to keep the slurs clear, but the upper one is more comfortable.

(ee) The *sf* is missing in the autograph.